SEASONS

A Year of Poetry and Other Essays

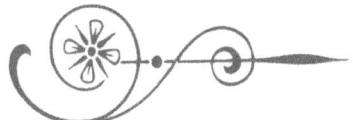

Vanessa Dove

Seasons

A Year of Poetry and Other Essays

Copyright © Vessel Publishing LLC, 2020.

All rights reserved. Except as permitted under U.S. Copyright Act of 1976, no part of this publication may be reproduced, distributed, or transmitted in any form or by any means, or stored in a database or retrieval system, without the prior written permission of the publisher.

Dove, Vanessa

1st edition

ISBN: 978-1-7360840-0-7

Cover Design by Mattias Fridh

Interior Layout by Femigraphix

Proofread and edited by Vessel Publishing in-house editing

Author Photo by Teresa

Printed in Northern California, USA

Vessel Publishing

To all my teachers, living and dead. And to the friend who told me the exaltation is in the writing, not in being read.

"In the beginning was the Word. And the Word was with God. And the Word was God."
John 1:1

TABLE OF CONTENTS

SPRING
A SWEET ACHE. 1
    Dear Reader, ... 2
    A Season of Aching 3
    Home. 4
    Sweet Thing. 5
    Minding one's business. 6
    Playtime. 7
    Men as Objects of Furniture 8
    Floralia: A Festival of Flowers. 9
    La Petite Mort. 11
    A Collection of Hazy Things. 12
    Surya: Devotional Poems to the Sun 14
    Summer Peaches. 16
    13 Lucky Affirmations 17
    Off to the Farmers Market. 18
    Another Poem Denouncing Stoicism 19
    Touch. 20
    Brown Girl 21
    Union. 22
    And Then There's Hope. 23
    Outbound 24
    Selected Plague Entries. 25
    Startling Truths. 29

SUMMER
LONG AND HOT. 31
    Summer's Conception. 32
    Selected Entries from Love Letters 33
    About Citrus 36
    Androphilia 37

Butterflies of the Night 38
Of Gods and Animals 39
Summer's Contempt. 40
Wolf. 41
A Toast 42
Her. 43
Good Little Churchgirl. 44
Autopsy Report. 45

AUTUMN
MEAT AND POTATOES. 46
    A Proper Introduction 47
    A Musing and Unwoven essays 50
    Essays on the moon 53
    Essay On the Color Blue 56
    An Essay on Belief and Fear 59
    Concussion 62
    24. 63
    What to Say to Break Up When You Don't Know What to Say
    64
    Essays on writing 65
    Outro. 67

WINTER
READ THESE AT MY FUNERAL. 68
    This is The End of The Vessel 69
    Funeral Etiquette 71
    Selected Confessions 72
    6 Letters from the dead 74
    A Eulogy for Spring. 77
    A Eulogy for Summer 79
    An Ode to Death 80
    Final Thoughts 81

Acknowledgements 83
About the Author. 84

SPRING
A sweet ache.

Dear Reader,

If you're reading this, I wrote this for you.
I want you naked and alone,
unmasked and completely yourself.
This is the best thing you could ever choose to be.
Read me when you're alone and it's dark.
Read me when you are afraid.
Read me when you need a sliver of hope.
If you're reading this, just know it's not too late to turn the page.

A Season of Aching

An ache
is an inner cry
to be touched with tenderness.

There is an ache to every season
and a season for every ache.

We ache for our collective wasted potential. Should have, could have, would have.

This ache longs to be released
and cries to be filled.

There are seasons of aching in all of us:
springs full of wanting, unraveling, regret, and rawness,

This was an aching summer that burned too bright and too hot before fading into dull embers of a glazed over autumn.

Home

Home is where the horses are.
Down the red dirt road
where the barn dogs howl and yip until the goats come home.
A place where rainfall makes the rivers bleed,
where the trees dance,
where the wind blows,
and where that big bowl of sky never ends.

Sweet Thing

Cherries and dates for breakfast
because I want my mornings to start sweet.

i used to want to feel like a peach
soft, ripe velvet on the fingers.

Minding one's business

I am a businesswoman
in the business of being a body.
In the business of being disastrously explicit.

Being busy being oneself is no part time job.
It is the only employment that lasts past death
and comes Regret Free guaranteed.

Playtime

My army of cyborg wives
are always ready to invade
the land of milk and honey

look! a hedonist!
yes. it is true what they say
indulgence is an artform

Mindless binging is for animals
but for us holy vessels,
there is sacred debauchery.

Men as Objects of Furniture

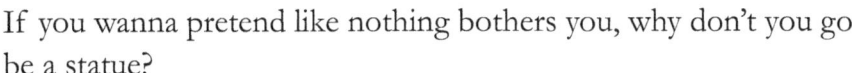

If you wanna pretend like nothing bothers you, why don't you go be a statue?
Better yet,
> *be my kitchen countertop.*

A smooth and hard cold, like granite. Men as objects of furniture.

Men as monuments without significance.
> *Monuments of men meant to be toppled.*

Men are better as pieces of marble: To be lovingly cut, to expose veins. This is necessary and desirable. Men as objects of furniture.

Floralia: A Festival of Flowers

I.
Prayers to her anchor me.
This white lotus heart of mine keeps on spinning and spinning and spinning.
I am graceless without the divinity of the flowers:
crowning me in bliss and
burying me in peace.

II.
There is a flower for everything:
Roses are the breath of the gods, they say.
But I know all flowers have divinity.
My god is Queen of the Poppies
She is the Lover of Apples
and the Mother of Relaxation

III.
Advice on charming me:
when you go to the florist,
scan the room.
Your eyes will pause
and you'll gaze at the flowers that remind you of me.

Those are the ones that I want.

IV.
Encircled in earth
You are the fruits
You are the trees
You are the garden
You are the bees.

V.
You don't have to overthink or control your way into blossoming.
Dance, celebrate, and ritual your way there.
Surround yourself with positive people.
You have the energy.
Time is on your side
and the seasons walk with you.
And sometimes,
we blossom while we sleep

La Petite Mort

I am so pleased I am going to pass out.

The peak of ecstasy is when I feel most full of power.

Ecstasy is the simultaneous fulfillment and release of desire.

It is many little deaths.

It is many excitements.

You are an excitement.

You are wild dancing around the fire.

You are the point of no return when the plane door is bolted shut.

A Collection of Hazy Things

I want to speak in windchimes and laugh in breezes.
Getting felt up by the wind always made me sing.

I'll dream for you. My dreams are big enough for the both of us. My dreams are big enough for the whole world. And the world is mine. One night I submerged myself in warm water. Under banana leaves, palm fronds, and moonlight and dreamt. Los Angeles is a place for people who dream. Heaven is wet and warm and sticky. It's a place in the rainforest with butterflies and dappled light.

I like to stare at the full moon till my eyes water.
I like to stare at the full moon till the white turns blue.

I keep getting carried away by my daydreams. They are the cobwebs. I am the fly.
They are words tucked further inside than I have reach. They are memories my knuckles have petrified over. They keep reaching out from within and touching me. I can't look away.

I only long to read poetry where I have to stop every few lines to sigh and squirm and feel. It's like I walk around with a cloud on my head. And while I'm delighted to be in the midst of something so soft and hazy, I want to see!

I'm so vain I found a way to mystify my vanity, but I mystify everything. These memories are soaked in so much light I want to live in them. Where I want to be?

In a room with wicker and pottery the color of camel.

Bossa-nova plays softly in the pre-noon sunlight and then there's him.

Surya: Devotional Poems to the Sun

I feel most at peace when the day is being born.
At 7 AM in the morning,
when he has just awoken,
it looks like heaven arrived outside my window.

I saw god peak out from behind the clouds today.
His light is the warmest hello.
The sun feels like a love letter.

At high noon,
the sun demands worship.
It beats down its rays
on the pavement,
through glass,
on my skin.
When it shines like that, we drip.

I wish I could be as rosy as the sky is when the sun sleeps.
Rosy thoughts and rosy voices.

His death is the most glorious of deaths.
The crossroads of earth and sky
mark his grave.

He is buried there every day.
The heavens sigh and mourn
in shades of gold and red.
All for Him.

Summer Peaches

The summer sun nodded and watched carefully every time I climbed the peach tree at our first house. With my books, I'd carefully climb up, scraping my knees and fingers on the bark. I'd sprawl out on the branches, limbs long, becoming weightless.

With pride and love that beamed, Mr. Sun showered my skin and the words on the pages with lazy bands of light. The leaves whispered in poetry every time the breeze came by.

13 Lucky Affirmations

I will hit my mark.
Even if I am unsure, I will hit my mark
Even if I disappoint myself, I will hit my mark
Even if I get rejected, I will hit my mark
Even if I'm insecure, I will hit my mark
Even if I'm sick, I will hit my mark
Even if I mess up, I will hit my mark
Even if I feel vulnerable, I will hit my mark
Even if I tell myself I can't, I will hit my mark
Even if the sun doesn't shine, I will hit my mark
Even if I fall short, I will hit my mark
Even if the sky is falling, I will hit my mark
Even if I don't know what comes next, I will hit my mark.

Off to the Farmers Market.

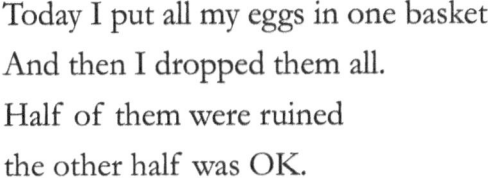

Today I put all my eggs in one basket.
And then I dropped them all.
Half of them were ruined
the other half was OK.

Another Poem Denouncing Stoicism

Dear sun,
You are of flesh and blood,
not stone and mountain.
Stone face.
Opaque face.
My door only opens
when one knocks with enthusiasm.

Touch

I can't figure out how to stop scarring my hands.
Also can't figure out how to stop touching either.
Maybe that's my problem: I'm going to touch the whole world.
A world without touch? Death.

Brown Girl

Brown girl with stars in her eyes
and butterflies in her mouth.
silver waves for hair
and corals for lips.

Brown girl
both the sea serpent and the snake charmer.
You were born with good luck
and visionary sight.

Brown girl
You are coiled up on the lap of the moon
Joy is woven in your hair
and resilience is your birthright

Union

When you remember that every breath is a prayer,
that is yoga.
When you remember the time is always now,
that is yoga.
When you remember wholehearted devotion to spirit,
that is yoga.
When you remember the real you is stainless and unbroken,
that is yoga.

And Then There's Hope

Your presence is your present.

I no longer wish to stumble my way through happiness.
I no longer wish to stumble my way through life.

Every day, I get to be more.
Every day, I fall forward.

The fun thing about being an adult
is you get to choose when you break the rules.

Outbound

Time to head west where the ocean lives,
where they are open hearts and open-ended letters,
long teary-eyed yawns and lazy stretches under a hazy glow of afternoon sun.
I trace shapes on your skin with my fingertips.
Every freckle is a star.
There is a home for me on earth.
There is happiness that stays
and hope that never leaves.

Selected Plague Entries

March 2020

I was too busy being traumatized to notice the day spring was born. She came on a Thursday, during the plague, with little fanfare. (The world has come back to eat itself. Mouth to tail.) I finally dusted myself off and I stand square in the light of clarity, ready for whatever happens now. I've had shit stolen from me my whole life. This is nothing to me. The Old World was never promised to us.

And maybe, when this is all over, I'll be and make art so beautiful no one will be able to look away.

It's 10:35 PM and I can't stop craving sugar and chocolate and sex. The moon still shines. I am alright. I will be alright.

I've cut most of my hair off. Week 3 and I broke the law and fled to a barber shop in the next city to buzz off most of what was left of my hair. I'm all for a DIY but I'd do anything to not be ugly.

I don't want to go back. I want to leave and never come back. I feel my time in this chapter of my life expiring, every second, every day. This place is my home. This place is my heart. But it is not my future. This little city was never enough for me.

I want a life lived recklessly. They said, go right? Now I need to make a left. They said, conversations aren't canceled? I say, keep your conversations! I want to speak his body language -fluently. They said, phone calls aren't canceled? I say, your phone calls can go to hell. I wanna fuck. They said, stay home? I say, now is the time to go out in the streets and rip all my clothes off!

April 2020

I don't count the days, I live them. All I want to do right now is swim. It's one of those days where the sun and ocean conspire and the beach calls out to you from the coast and if you don't listen by the time the sun sleeps you know you missed out. I just want to lay on a big warm rock with a platter of figs and cheese and the love of my life's hand on my thigh.

Despite all the chaos, I'm happy. It's life in the eye of a hurricane. There is contentment here. Today I laid in bed... fully sank into my pillow... and watched the clouds roll by outside my window. I can't remember the last time I did that. I really don't want to go back now.

On second thought, the plague has been terrible for me. I deal with stress by withdrawing and in a plague one must withdraw. So I have just withdrawn then withdrawn from being told to withdraw and then withdrawn from that? Such a terrible feedback loop.

May 2020

I live in my own bubble and it's better this way. And then the city burned to the ground. My path remains the same. Ah, looting! Such riveting street theater! I didn't go to the protest because I don't feel like getting my face bashed in today. I've already been knocked out twice and you know what they say about the number 3. The public continues to displease me. Even I can admit things have gotten out of hand. In all honesty some of the chaos is entertaining. Some of it is terrifying.

He's dead, not suffering. We're suffering, not dead. Being at one with the world has never looked so ugly. The world bleeds and pisses and shits.

And now come the bombs. Just kidding. Only slightly. Knock on wood. I'd be a liar if I said I wasn't afraid. This isn't what I meant when I said I like wild. I want to get off this ride now. I don't like this world anymore. Excuse me, I need to go throw things now.

Sad news: I went to the protest and all I did was cry. I'm not the angry 20-something-year-old I used to be. Too passionate to not be in the streets. Too riveting to not be in the streets. Revolution is coming and it smells like teargas. March. Rest. March. Rest. March rest. March rest. March rest. This is my heartbeat. The moon is our witness. Call me a lightning bolt. I've screamed enough for the whole year.

I met a saint today. She called herself a prophet of God. She told me I have a warm heart and to not be afraid of taking that leap. God wants me to take that leap. Speaking of god, I need a goddamn miracle.

I'm starting to see gods everywhere. The sun, the moon, the waving palms that line the next block over. Everyday there's a rainbow wrapping it's neck and tail around the sun. Father sky. Ouroborus.

June 2020

There was a plague once that made people dance themselves to death. In this plague, we amuse ourselves to death.

Confession: I go out and take care of thousands of people in the streets to fill the hole. Which hole? *That* hole.
Bad news: it didn't fill the hole.

Ah, another day in hell. No -not hell. Just another day with *you all.* My life is great, it's outside the door where Hell lives. Outside is the 7th layer of Hell and we are plagued by lightning, fire, and virus.
More bad news: Violence and terrible weather will continue. More deaths today. More deaths tomorrow. Here we go again.

Startling Truths

Life is a race to the bottom. No one has ever been good enough for the poetry I write about them. Bugs will drown themselves in any pool. Even a million dollar home in Beverly Hills isn't spared their carelessness. Spirituality doesn't have a favorite outfit. Every moment you spend not moving the body is a moment closer to death. There would be no sex without death. Naivety and low standards equal an explosive combination. All my female heroes had guns. My dad would have loved me more if I was a son. Maybe if my grandpa hadn't picked cotton or woken up in trees after getting blown up in Korea, he wouldn't have raised such an insecure son. My dad's just mad he had a white lookin' mama who wasn't actually white and the moment she opened her mouth she became Other. Parents are things to be outgrown. To be a woman is invisibility. To be a black woman is …

I don't have relationships, I get struck by lightning. Everything I'm getting better at requires deeper levels of vulnerability from me and I hate it. Everyone's looking out for themselves and friendship is a luxury. That's what no one told me. Or maybe they did and I couldn't hear them over the sound of my own hope. Sometimes spring sucks. It's OK.

There's always next year.

That's the thing about seasons:

There's always another one.
    And they always come back.

SUMMER
Long and Hot.

Summer's Conception

Cherries and bong rips.
That's how you know summer's coming.

Summer always comes twice.
The days are really nights.
Twice baked and bathed
in golden starlight

Summer's born. What need do we have of Night?
For we have the loving grace of Our Holy Star
The Lord
All day long.

Selected Entries from Love Letters

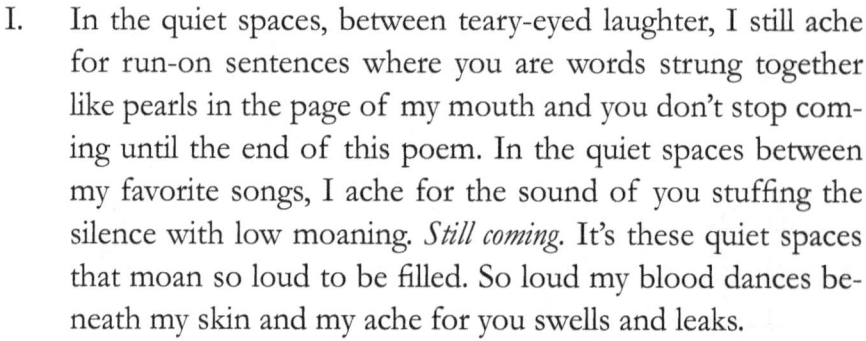

I. In the quiet spaces, between teary-eyed laughter, I still ache for run-on sentences where you are words strung together like pearls in the page of my mouth and you don't stop coming until the end of this poem. In the quiet spaces between my favorite songs, I ache for the sound of you stuffing the silence with low moaning. *Still coming.* It's these quiet spaces that moan so loud to be filled. So loud my blood dances beneath my skin and my ache for you swells and leaks.

II. I am unlike any of your other women. If she gives you a rose, I give you the garden. If she gives you flames, I'll give you the sun. Should another give you a river, I'll bring the whole ocean. She is a sign post, her body may be landmarks, but I am the path.

III. I want to orbit you. I don't want to be a satellite, but I will be your Moon. There are many fish in the sea and I want to toss a silver hook in it just for you. I want to consume you and then become you. The vision of your face lingers in the bright spaces of the day; shining light and benevolently haunting unoccupied spaces in my mind. You too, are a son of the gods. You are of them and they are in you. You are a door I opened and found gods in. There is no place where you start and they or I stop. You are deathless.

IV. I can't stop thinking about finding you again when I'm better. I have nowhere to go but upward and onward. Love makes me shiny on the outside. Like platinum not tin foil. I don't know what it is about it that makes me wanna throw away everything. To hurl all my trinkets in the streets. So I have more space for you.

V. This is a love letter but it was never love. It's just the way my body responds to, hungers for, demands you. It is not love. It's the feeling of dozens of lightning bolts being birthed inside. It is not love, I'm just a thrill seeker. This is an *almost love letter*. Another almost. In the house of the spirit of Almost, I dance with the memory of you. Your features slivers of light flitting at the edges of my vision. I keep dreaming with my eyes open. Willingly. Longingly. You are not real and that's OK.

If I thought of you all day, does that mean I thought of you once? Or 900 times for every minute I spent awake? I even thought about you in my dreams this morning. Even in a dream, you were busy. Even in a dream, you still couldn't be mine.

VI. I will not lie: I want to think about you. I want to hold the image of your face, like a statue. Worship it, get on my knees, and prostrate myself. I am the altar girl. You are my idol. I like to shiver *pleasurably*. The thought of you kidnapping me excites me. Rapture: To be carried away. A mystical experience in which the spirit begins to stretch outside the body. *To stand outside oneself.* In this intoxication, I indulge until I ascend my body and come back an animal. No thinking. Just sensing. Obsession is possession by lesser spirits. If your vessel is cracked, they'll drive you mad. I'm blessed with a big vessel. Narrow hole, wide mouth. I've always loved giving myself over to it.

VII. Don't be fooled by the calm, love. I'm burning too much to be a safe landing strip.

About Citrus

I.
Today, my favorite fruit is a Tangelo. The love child of Tangerine and Pomelo. I love the color of her insides. I can't help putting as much as I can in my mouth. The more I eat the more she squirts. I like it when it dribbles down my chin. It's so juicy it's intoxicating. And the tartness is enchanting. It's a ritual to lick my fingers after and all the sticky places in between.

II.
I'll put lemon on anything. I'll suck on one just to shock my mouth. Lemon says, "Wake up wake up! The day is bright and the air is crisp!"

Androphilia

I've always admired men's carelessness, in some way or another. To be careless. Carefree. It made me envious. Being envious made me surprised. When I'm surprised, I'm out of control so I ignored it and cared until I couldn't keep carrying -I meant caring.

Butterflies of the Night

Moths are nothing but flying curses. Butterflies that ruminated in the night too long and lost the blessings of Father Sun. They could not see his greatness so he cursed them to wander the night, burning themselves to death trying to fill the hole his brightness left. I crushed a moth that flew too close to me. I didn't hate it, it confused me. It annoyed me. It chased after me like I was starlight.
Oh.

I am votive candlelight in the dark.

And then I remembered all the men and women I crushed like moths too.

Of Gods and Animals

There is no tension as exquisite as remaining maskless. Let others continue the show. Something animal in me opens its eyes. Animal and god. Eros lives inside a sliver of our insides and uses our eyes as quivers. In tension, I admit, I have shot multiple men and women. Weapon of choice?

A gaze like flaming arrows. *That gaze.* I am looking at you with the face of a god and you are looking at me with the face of a god. But who has seen the face of gods and angels and not wept in fright? There is no loving without leaving and letting go. And so the comfortable void comes creeping. Negative space left in the wake of blinding eye beams and an inflamed heart.

Summer's Contempt

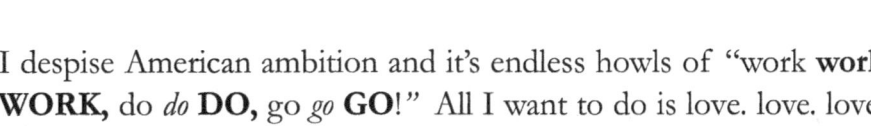

I despise American ambition and it's endless howls of "work **work WORK,** do *do* **DO,** go *go* **GO!**" All I want to do is love. love. love. To drape myself over a chaise at a beach with sand so warm it burns. To do nothing but write and love and lounge. When I think of the pressure to choose ambition over love, something inside me cracks.

I despise how short sighted most men's notion of beauty is. I am a *connoisseur* of beauty! Men hear this and say, they too, are connoisseurs of beauty. I always scoff. They're just connoisseurs of what makes their dick hard. There's a difference. We are not the same.

Wolf.

I am afraid of you.
Not because you are a violent man,
but because of the ferocity of hunger I feel when I think of you
see you
touch you.
It reminds me: I am not, nor have I ever been, domesticated.

A Toast

Raise your glass and let's make a toast. I'll start:
I toast to beauty. I toast to beautiful women that are silky, shiny like satin and new sheets, with highlight like high beams. I toast to the beauty of mid morning sunshine and the crunch and squeak of virgin snow under bootheels. To coming so hard my eyes water, second chances, and tomorrows. I toast to soft tinkly laughter and brown women with glowing skin who love their culture.

This poem is a toast to velvet. To attractive strangers and extraordinary encounters. May we never forget moments so beautiful and so ecstatic our spirits dance outside our bodies. Let us toast to our dream girls. Let us toast to sunlit, teary-eyed yawns. Let us toast to the body, the living temple. Let us toast to the inherent beauty of ourselves.

    Cheers to that.

Her.

The woman I've been consumed with my whole life is intense and deep like me. When I'm with her she has this way of engaging all that intensity and channeling it into focusing on me. I just want to bathe in the light of her attention at all times. When she talks, I feel like I'm the only person in the world. I **used to be** jealous of **her** girlfriend. I **was** jealous of her cat. Even jealous of the floor she walk**ed** on.

Good Little Churchgirl

I worship Beauty and Pleasure.
They are my gods
-and I am a pious woman.
I pray for and to them.
Life without sensation, devoid of indulgence,
devoid of the light of beauty
is godless.
And I must shun the ungodly.
Hell is a place on earth and it's spelled u-g-l-y.

Autopsy Report

Name of Deceased: <u>Vanessa Dove</u>
Age of Death: <u>24 years old</u>

Cause of Death: <u>heart failure</u>
Hour of Death: <u>dead on arrival</u>

My heart died this morning because I woke up and just fucking flatlined. This comes after an extended period of disconnect and heart closure during The Great Year of the Plague. This cause of death is common but preventable. Symptoms of heart closure include: moody outbursts, angry muttering, frantic thoughts that nobody cares about you, ghosting, and going on blocking sprees. Risk factors for heart closure include: shitty friends, global plague, isolation, racism, grind culture, and capitalism. The compounding effect of multiple risk factors is enough to disregulate the heart system which over time can lead to congestive heart failure.

R.I.P.

AUTUMN
Meat and Potatoes

A Proper Introduction

My name is Vanessa Dove, like the bird. I'm a third-generation cult baby and I really like horses. I like to pretend the me of yesterday never existed. There is only the me of today. I am a wonderful person to dream with. If I don't wheeze or snort when I laugh at your joke it means you're really not that funny and I just feel bad so I laugh so it doesn't get awkward. If someone makes me nervous, I think about them with their skin ripped off. Nothin' attractive about that. I certainly don't have the urge to overperform for a skinless human!

If I was a balloon, I'd be a yellow balloon and I'd be shaped like a perfect sphere or a heart. Not those weird almost-circles or whatever the hell those traditional balloons have to be to be accepted at parties. I still think Portland and Seattle are the same place, but don't tell anyone from there I said that.

I'm still not exactly sure what happens when I eat peanut butter. I just know my mind leaves my body after the first spoonful and goes somewhere so intensely pleasurable and doesn't bother coming back till half the jar is gone and I have a stomach ache. What's my diagnosis? I don't know, but I really fucking like peanut butter.

The top of chihuahuas' skulls are shaped like a marble and it makes me uncomfortable. I've never liked little dogs. Their voices are shrill and they're usually stuck up. I'm terrified I'd accidentally step on one because I don't look down when I walk and I'd feel it's little spine crunch and snap underneath my foot.

I can't stand looking at photos of myself meditating. It makes Shallow Me bitter that someone can be so peaceful without giving a fuck what they look like. I just want to hold hands with all the different versions of myself and dance madly in circles until we whirl so fast we blur together. I just wanna hold hands with someone and cast deep loving gazes and be kind to each other until one of us dies. I want to curl up into a ball and make myself as small as physically possible and then be held to eternity.

I don't like that I can't see my own eyes with my own eyes and that I can never really watch my own back. I do like looking at myself with other people's eyes. I also like when men smell like a dark leather saddle left on a wooden post in the sun in a field of black pepper and clove blossoms. I like men who smell like freshly soaped and washed skin with a hint of clean linen. Simple. Clean. To the point. I like that which I am not.

I like being unexpected. I like ownership and I like control. I like being intellectually provocative. I like getting into a flow and losing track of time. I like reaching back in time to dead versions of myself to shake their corpses until they give me something good to write.

Primary colors make me shudder. Who needs loud colors when you have a loud mouth? I'm a queer person who doesn't identify with queer culture. I like and respect rainbows as a natural phenomenon, but as a personal aesthetic, I think they're a goddamn trainwreck. I prefer beige and variations of bone, rust, and camel.

I want to be as beautiful as my grandma was before the world ruined her. I don't hate myself but when I'm frustrated, I think I do.

I sleep with my back to the wall because it feels safe. I can't function on less than nine hours of sleep. I read books so I feel less alone. I'm not afraid to die but I am afraid of pain. I meditate, so I remember who I am.

If we never speak again, this is everything you need to know. I am a humble daughter of earth. I am nothing compared to her terror. I dream of celestial violence. I dream of being branded with lightning fire. Where does the wind sleep when it's tired of roaming the earth and waters? Does lightning bury herself or is she content with just brushing the surface with her fingers? I am a willow alone in a valley. I am lightning's first kiss.

For all my charm and social grace, there is a part of me that will always remain explosive and impulsive. Reactive and rebellious. I am a spitfire or a stick of dynamite. Some days I can't tell. I am a braid. I am woven of many threads. Many colors. Some stained. Some brilliant. I am a knot that won't come undone. Fantasies that haunt. Blood that boils. I am the overripe fruit. A peach on a branch left dangling under July suns and August moons.

This has been and always will be, The Vanessa Show.

A Musing and Unwoven essays

An anarchist once called me an herb scientist. I called them the most faithful person I've ever met. I like being around revolutionaries because I like being around faith.

If I ever become paralyzed, just shoot me. Pull the plug, because I can't take a life without this body. I can't take a half life. I'm tired of almost, of "ehs", "I guesses", and "good enoughs." Fuck good enoughs and half-assed efforts and second and third place. I tire of this country that reeks with the stench of conformity and despair. Of mindless wealth and boring men.

For the longest time, the sight of skeletons used to frighten me. Even though I'm a walking skeleton who was born into a family of walking skeletons. Even though I went to schoolhouses filled with walking skeletons of all shapes and sizes and I live on a whirling ball with 7 billion skeletons all jostling for space. I think it was because I wanted to believe The Lie. The Lie that we're fancy animals with fancy clothes and fancy faces and there's nothing primal about us. There's nothing fancy about bones.

In another life, I was a jester. Head of the clown show. Jestering is for *professionals only!* It's no fools work to be a fool. In fact, it's the fools duty to deliver bad news. Real fools don't wear masks. I'm afraid if you take this mask off parts of my skin will get peeled away with it. Here's a riddle: how many masks were you wearing the last time you spoke to someone you love?

Skin, I say to you, stop being a wall. And it ceased.

I am the beach. I am the sandbank. I am the birds that skitter and the children who laugh and shriek. If I had it my way, I'd live at that bathhouse near the beach and take seven showers a day. I clutch my quartzes from the bathhouse when I want a dose of palm sized purity. I changed my whole lifestyle just so I could look like an angel. I want to look like I was touched lovingly my whole life by a ceramicist.

O, beauty! I wonder about the day I see someone so beautiful I lose consciousness and pass out. Blame Stendhal. You can't trust beautiful people or so they say. This is probably sound advice. I, the spokesperson of the beautiful people of the world, am well aware of our general unreliability. That's because there's always someone else. I'm so popular, I have to beat them off with a stick.

Here I am and I'm ready to consume. Here I am, entertain me! Here I am and I'm ready to create another thing to be consumed and forgotten. But you can never forget this. I am This. I am That. My gifts are ghosts and that is my gift.

Please, friend, unfasten yourself from that cross. In the name of the heavens, unbind yourself! Devote the day to unwinding that knot no hands can untangle. These knots that are born, bound, and threaded in all the weary moments you realize that life is suffering. Knots wound from shelved moments of intimacy and bad endings. Weave necklaces from your grief where every bead is a disappointment and never run out of jewelry. "The graces rather look upon that which is adorned." said Sappho the Great. We, the scorched, wear our burn marks proudly. Quilting a story of sins and sacrifices worth sharing to the world. I am an animal selling its inner turmoil. You are an animal consuming the inner landscape of another animal.

Essays on the moon

It's proven science that people commit more crimes when she comes out. Maybe that's why they say she drives people crazy. She ain't all that. Haven't you heard? She just steals the light from the Sun and calls it her own. *He made her.* I've never actually seen that but if They said she did it, I believe it. Actually come to think of it, I've never seen them alone in the same room before. Are they really in love, Sun and Moon? I wish I could ask her why she's okay always coming second. I've never thought to myself *I want to be someone's night.* I have been someone's silent witness.

Everyone that's been in or on her says she's cold and spacey. But if that's true, why have men spent their whole lives training to be good enough just to be in her orbit? I know the real her. She's really a big ball of fire. I know so because of that blue glaze of an aura she gets sometimes when she's full. Sadly, she only shows her whole self once a month. The rest of the time's spent oscillating between hiding and giggling. She really is beautiful when you look at her. I wish I saw more than just her parts. She's tireless with all that starting over. I guess you could say the moon is deathless that way. I'm just glad she hasn't given up on me yet.

Strange Fact: We know more about the moon than we do the sea. Another night, another allegory. To be honest, it annoyed me how much she came around. Every damn night. No, not annoyed, just indifferent. I slept on her like men slept on me. *Oh*. Can't know what you're not awake for.

Many moons ago. What a wonderful phrase. What a wonderful moon. No one asked her to look after us when we sleep and still she rises to the occasion. I'm going to throw my masks at her and make hangers of the stars. Can that which has no eyes see? There's nothing quite like the ritual of gazing lovingly. O, moon of moons. There are many moons and then there is you. The moon is for soft men who like to hide.

At night's end, when she goes home past the mountain, do you think the moon laughs at us? What is the word for an internal snarl? I don't know but I do know the moon is absolutely, undeniably mad. I say mad with an internal snarl. Quick, somebody, shoot down the moon! Raving and rising and all that *goddamn watching!* The moon is an absolute demon, the worst of the bunch. In true demonic fashion she just sits there and stares until you scream and rip all your hair out. It's absolutely mad, the absurdity of it all. This spirit has no face. This spirit is a god.

Today I feel like ripping all my hair out. Frantic for the moon to come back because the sun keeps burning me tender & raw. Sun is too busy being a Star to notice small little me. It has been so many nights it has almost been a year and I still think of you. Moon help me. It takes approximately one night for me to fall in lust. I hate the architects who build houses on hills because now it's harder to see you. You know I don't do long distance, love. I am nothingness; I am cursed. I am nothingness; I am freed. Call me a heretic for writing about the moon in the middle of the day. Drag this crescent sliver of a heart outside my body. Moon heart. I've got a bone white moon for a blood red heart. This heart beats bloody red. This heart eats itself and snarls and claws until it's sinews snap.

I want to hold her hand. I want to touch the places in her body that cave in. She will never let me. She will always gaze at me from beyond the hills, with pity. I will always want her. I will always drift between love and hate. Moody like your mother. Oh, is it twilight? Time to turn inside out. Moon in the guts. Save me, brother moon. Maybe if I thought of you as much as I thought of him, I might be less mad. Do you shine on him too? I'm jealous. Thank the heavens you shine and show up the same for everyone. An eclipse for me but bands of moonlight for him? Now I have to kill you, that's all. Murdering the moon? Moon murder. How mad.

Hello mother moon, I'm your curly headed daughter and I love you very much. Have you heard my whispers at empty crossroads in the witching hour? Wild haired and maniacal. Brown like spaces in between day's hard shaft. I paid the spirits in garlic and coins. Now death likes me and cloves grow along the spiral at the center of the road. The moon is for me and what's mine belongs to the moon. We are lucky to be called yours. Us lost daughters who roam the earth.

The past twelve lives I've lived I spent wandering. There's no wind on the surface of the moon so there's nothing to wipe away footprints. If I counted every step I took in every life I've lived would they make a billion? That's billion with a B. I am deathless with a D. Unfortunately I still bleed. The moon bleeds too.

Sex is for witches because sex is for coming and coming is magic. Magic is for dying and magic is for birth. This vessel was built for ashes and seawater. Coming and crying are the same thing. Same sea, different stream. Drains are for dumping things and masks are for the gutter. All gutters drain to the Moon's house. N is for nighttime. Night is for the naked. And the moon is for me. I'm sorry you thought otherwise.

Essay On the Color Blue

Blue is actually black. Black so dark that it's blue. There is only Black. There is only blue that bleeds into night. There is only blue that fades into morning. The sun rises in gold to be draped in blue. I promise if you go out to see every sunset and sunrise you will be happier. I'm happier when the sky is clear and the blue is so intense you can get lost in it. It's limitless. Question: Is the sky blue or is it just one big bowl made to hold color?

Blue is just a blanket word for many shades and hues of blue, all with their own energy. Blue is an inherently medicinal color. It's a good idea to get blue on your plate. Blue foods are high in anthocyanins and they are good for your heart. In the Mahayana Buddhist tradition, images of the Medicine Buddha, a being of great compassion, commonly depict him as a blue lapis lazuli or surrounded by lapis colored light. Using this image as an object of meditation is encouraged because concentrating on it creates internal calm and peace. I don't know if every person who stares at this will actually be calmed down. I imagine someone having a nervous breakdown and somehow I don't think showing them a statue that happens to be colored blue or made out of some precious jewel would be helpful in that exact moment. Essentially, color therapy isn't a substitution for immediate distress management. That being said, I really love meditating on this shade of blue and maybe you might love it too. Deep blue just has this way of enveloping you entirely. I imagine this is what it's like in the ocean. Not near the seabed but also not at the surface. A liminal space. Maybe that's where the attraction comes from. It's an attractive color because of what it represents. It's suggestive of possibility and hope. As a feeling, it's calming because it's welcoming and protective. Deep blue has a way of providing a feeling of being sheltered.

How many naturally blue things can you count? There is blue in lightning, in fire, and full moonlight. It is in glaciers and rivers and storm clouds. It's so contradictory that both water and fire can be blue. Or maybe that's just because of the binary we've put on those two elements as being inherently opposite.

I never understood why people call being sad "the blues." The Classical Dictionary of the Vulgar Tongue describes blue as to be terrified or disappointed. It also goes on to say that the phrase "blue devils" means to be in low spirits. The phrase comes from stories of menacing spirits that would supposedly torment chronic alcoholics into psychosis. I've never gotten alcohol poisoning, but I have seen evil spirits dressed up as people wearing blue.

I am not in control of how blue is used. I am not in control of anything. Control is an illusion. So are most things. In this place, blue is for bruises, law, and order. It's for police, garlanded in shields and stars and bullets and blue. The boys in blue dig their bootheels in. They shove blue face down in the dirt and spit on it. It's blue gone muddy. It's blue gone rogue. It's blasphemous that such a pure color would be used as the symbol for something so callous. I guess if there's such a thing as color therapy there would be such a thing as color warfare. It makes me think about how pure and beautiful fresh snow and glaciers are until people stomp on it and it goes grubby and grey.

Blue is just a phenomenon we experience internally because of our eyes and the flesh inside our heads. It is ultimately an eternal illusion; our personal and social interpretation of light. In knowing this, I wish colors didn't have to be political. I guess that's the price to pay for being human -or at least for living in the West. In reality, blue is neither hopeful nor sad. As such, it cannot be owned by any group; not spiritualists, not the police, and not even me. There is only light and our attempts at finding and defining it that have fallen short.

An Essay on Belief and Fear

Belief. That's a buzzword, especially in the New Age / neo-spiritual community. You can't talk about belief without talking about fear. Belief is the absence of fear -or rather, continuation despite the presence of fear. Where there is no belief, there is no progress. For me, there's nothing as terrifying as being ugly. I'm afraid I'll never be pretty like her. Pretty people get treated better. It's science. I believe beauty can save me. I believe beauty has saved me.

I believe if I don't make art, I'll die. I'm afraid what will happen if I can no longer write. I'm afraid I'll never find a muse that stays. Ultimately, I believe I am a normal functioning person but I am afraid I will always be this sensitive.

I choose to believe that true divinity is just unconditional love. I choose this specifically because of how afraid I am of how intensely I feel love. I'm afraid I've only known attachment and lust. I'm afraid no one will ever love me like I love them. This fear is insecure and corrosive.

When I'm on a plane and we land, sometimes the air pressure changes so quickly that I get migraines and they hurt so bad all I can think about is ending it. It makes me afraid of flying. Belief has its limits when it comes to the body. I read in a popular book once that if you believe you have a disease, you'll think your way into that. It said all diseases and disorders have roots in the mind. How toxic. Can you, in good faith, tell someone who got lung cancer because of their environment that they had no control over that they simply "thought" their way into radicalizing their own body so as to commit acts of terror against them?

The thought of not being more and having more than the people who wronged me is terrifying. There is no written guarantee that the people who hurt me, you, or anyone will get what's coming to them and that those of us who have been hurt will get justice. The reason why religion and spirituality can be so hypnotic and addictive is because they offer us the belief that everything will be alright in the end because God cares too much to let us suffer. It makes sense why Marx said "religion is the opium of the people." That's the thing about belief though; whether or not what is believed is real, it's a choice. By making that specific choice to believe, to surrender and rest in complete faith in things unseen, miracles can and do happen. I believe in many gods. I believe spirits walk among us. I believe not all ancestors are good. I believe we make our own luck. I believe success can be prepared for.

Not all beliefs are helpful. Like the belief that showing emotions and being open about your distress makes you weak. I believe in the freedom of weeping. I believe in getting on my knees.

I guess you could argue my belief is only partial because I'm still afraid I might be wrong about the world. It's a challenge to have complete faith in a place that is so chaotic and traumatic. I believe in armed self-defense. I believe all power to the people. I'm afraid of being stabbed with my own knife in a fight. There is no fear like the fear of walking alone downtown. Sometimes it seems impossible to have complete faith and belief as a woman. I believe her when she says he did it. I'm afraid we will never have a revolution. I'm afraid real justice takes lifetimes. Despite all this I still choose to believe the future is worth staying for. I would be lying if I said that this belief didn't grow organically deep down inside me, continuing on despite fire and blood and rain. I believe I was always meant for this. I believe I'll get what I want.

Concussion

I got thrown from a horse once. A blackout is a memorable event with nothing remembered. I screamed the names of god to save me. The reins had fallen, dragged and trampled under frightened hooves. We were both terrified, our hearts and hoofbeats thundering in unison. Just stay in the saddle. That's all I had to do. I grabbed at the silvery tufts of mane but they felt like bare threads and my fingers were swollen maggots squirming to get a grip. And then he made a sharp left and I flew off the saddle.

So much for stirrups. A powder blue sky peaked out from between the pine needles. That's the last thing I saw before the clanging of my body against the metal fence of the arena. Then darkness.

I woke up in the middle of a field, clenching palmfuls of dirt and sand. Watching thousands of grains bleed out from between my fingers back to the dust. From crown to toe, the entire left side of me was in searing pain. White hot fire pain. Then voices. Voices from beyond. From the fog. What fog? I don't know. Faces scrunched into concern and love, the faces of my mother and trainer became clear.

Did they drive my lifeless body from where I was thrown to the middle of the field? I asked myself. "How did I get here?"

"You walked."

That memory must've been knocked out of me. That's okay with me. The fog can keep it.

24

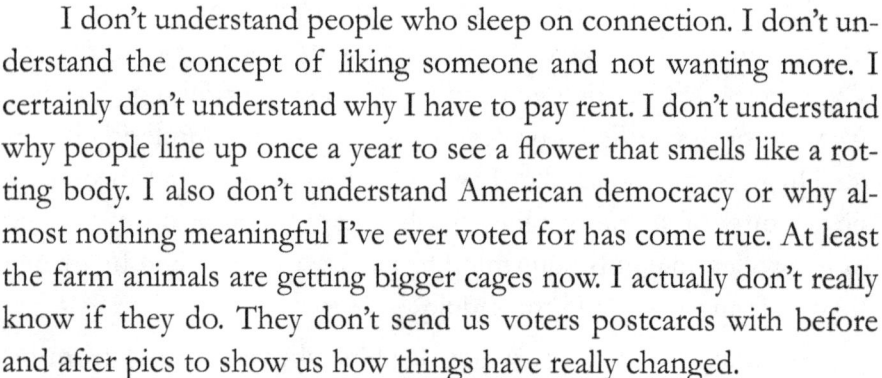

I don't understand people who sleep on connection. I don't understand the concept of liking someone and not wanting more. I certainly don't understand why I have to pay rent. I don't understand why people line up once a year to see a flower that smells like a rotting body. I also don't understand American democracy or why almost nothing meaningful I've ever voted for has come true. At least the farm animals are getting bigger cages now. I actually don't really know if they do. They don't send us voters postcards with before and after pics to show us how things have really changed.

I don't understand why deleting all my text threads feels so satisfying or why being pretty and mean gets me off. I don't understand why I'm still so greedy after six years of yoga, no dairy, and green juice. I do know I'm not the only one. Someone explain to me why bad things come in 3's

example: pandemic, police terror, and poverty.

What to Say to Break Up When You Don't Know What to Say

It's not you, it's my inner turmoil.

Actually, it's not me, it is you!

Everything about you displeases me, goodbye!

You bore me.

Error 404 cannot be found.

SIKE!

You're not terrible, I just don't want to write a book after being with you.

You don't inspire me.

You don't own your insecurities.

I don't want to sit on your face.

I don't like who I am when I'm with you.

I changed.

I never really wanted you, I just wanted something you had.

When you talk, my eyes want to roll all the way back in my skull and glaze over.

You have no purpose.

I'm a 9, you're a 1, and I just needed to make a 10.

Essays on writing

Novels, visions, and ideas keep knocking around inside my skull. Some of them fling themselves with such intensity I become possessed with the Spirit of the Word. It has always been this way. The spirit just comes out of me.

Someone once told me, "If you want to make a difference, write a book." I scoffed. What a ridiculous idea. And now, here I am. Trying to write poetry now is like trying to sing a melody written in a language I forgot. Dialect is self-expression. Maybe this time I need a translator. Is it me or is everyone a little off today? Maybe we're just not on the same wavelength. Maybe we're just tuned to different notes. Fuck, we even move different.

Being a writer is whoredom. To be an author, a poet, is to sell a piece of yourself to anyone with 15$ and a wifi connection. Publishing your work is giving birth to a baby and giving the baby away and having faith it'll be OK. It's out of my hands now. Like God making the human race and saying "Good luck! Call me if you need me but it's up to you now."

It's better to write about nonsense than date it. My advice as a publisher:

more painting, less whining

I write because I was never any good at painting. Writing has become a lens through which I see myself. It has also become the means through which I free myself. I write if I can't run. I write so I don't forget. I write so I don't have to talk to you. And I write so I don't lose myself. And I write to free myself. I write to take control of the story. I write so I can touch people from beyond the grave. I write so something of mine can outlive me. I write so I can have permanence. I write so I can give voice to the unspeakable. I write so I can make people laugh at my funeral.

I was born and then I became a writer.

The End.

Outro

Hey it's me again. I can't talk to you right now because I'm busy figuring out how to be better than I was last time. You missed me last season. I was open all spring and wide all summer. The last chapter of me was too open and I got dog-earred and bent. Lucky for me my heart my line didn't completely disconnect. Yet.

WINTER
Read these at my Funeral

This is The End of The Vessel

There were two things prophesied when I was born: She will be greatness

and then she will die.

Do not be alarmed that I have died! In reading this, you revived and suspended my consciousness for a moment. Do not be alarmed that I died because I consciously chose to live over and over again. I never wanted to die. Not once -even when I said I did. I just wanted to be free to live my purpose. Never hated myself either -even when I said I did. I was just frustrated with myself and didn't know how to say it or what to do about it -until I did. I always knew who I was. Life for me was a process of remembering and consciously choosing to pull back pieces of myself to make a whole. I made that choice repeatedly. Then forgot. Then remembered. The more I grew, the less I forgot.

Truthfully speaking, the only reason I'm writing this is so my parents don't kidnap my body and do weird shit with it like stuff it with sawdust or dress it like an Amish person. I want to be cremated with amber and my favorite herbs, then I want my ashes put in a treasure chest with all my gold jewelry and more herbs. It is **imperative** that I'm cremated while wearing a white crop top and white biker shorts. As some of you may have known, I had severe allergies most of my life and by the time I was 20 I had developed an allergy to normal sized T-shirts. In order to avoid anaphylactic shock, I only bought crop tops and tanks and would knot my big t-shirts and turtlenecks so my stomach could breathe. Please make sure my hair is slicked back the way I like it and I'm wearing layers of gold necklaces, hoops, and my toe rings and anklets.

I must be escorted out to the Pacific, tied to a cinder block, and then let go. Then comes the ceremonious weeping. Bonus points if anyone gets on their knees.

This is the end of the vessel. This vessel was built for Beauty. This vessel was built for Grace. This vessel was built for movement. This vessel was built with lightning and fire and this vessel was built with faith. This vessel was built for greatness. Out of this vessel came the voices of the gods.

Funeral Etiquette

No black lace, no bible reading, and no embarrassing stories. I understand that this is a heavy subject and funerals aren't really anyone's definition of "fun" but everyone should really try to be lighthearted, for my sake. It's what I want and my funeral is about nobody else but **me!** I pray for the people who only get recognition in death. Not I.

If you really want to know how I want my funeral to go, read my will. I prepared for my death when I was alive. You could say it was an extension of my chosen spiritual beliefs which hovered somewhere between Buddhist, Yogic, and non denominational. That and one perilous summer pushed me to plan the future. Real spirituality should prepare you for death. Death is inevitable. It is the only constant in life. I don't really want a single speaker or leader at my funeral but I do want there to be lively discussions about finding peace in death.

I would prefer if people wear monochromatic outfits, preferably beige. I want this to be a fashionable event. I don't want anyone to stress themselves out over it, but then again, it is my funeral and it's all about me and I want fashion!

If any etiquette is broken, especially the first three requests, you can be sure I will be rolling in my watery grave and I will come back as a spirit and fucking choke you.

Selected Confessions

I confessed these when I wrote them so I died with a light heart, but I have provided a select few for
you now for your entertainment and mild discomfort:

I was raised a Christian but I never prayed over my food at school.

The first place a woman let me take her clothes off was church.

All I ever wanted was to be dreamy, intense, and achingly beautiful. So beautiful it's hypnotic.

I don't know how not to wear my whole heart on my sleeve and right now my sleeve is on fire.

I wanted to start over so I shaved my head. I wanted to start over so I threw away all my shit. I wanted to start over so I moved 3000 miles away. I wanted to start over so I moved another 3000 miles away. When I want to start over, I go somewhere where no one knows my name.

I replaced the lyrics of all my favorite songs with my own writing so I could listen to myself over and over in a variety of genres. The definition of insanity is doing the same thing over and over in the same way and expecting the same results.

The most unloved part of my body is the outer corner of my left foot.

I lose track of time when I see myself in a mirror.

I'm really looking for a double of myself in another body.

The last man I dated I used like a Band-Aid and when it got itchy I ripped it off.

I didn't mean to disrespect anyone, I just wanted to consume all the best parts of them for myself.

I don't feel like being nice to myself today.

I feel like being a masochist today.

Objectifying men is sexy.

I like being a dirty girl with a clean face.

Violence sometimes excites me.

Men still elude me.

Humanity continues to disgust me.

Beauty still saves me.

Books still save me.

And then I met him.

And still, I want more.

6 Letters from the dead

I. Death came shining, warm and wet, and I crumbled like sand into it. She is softer than I thought she'd be. She doesn't leave a bad taste in my mouth or grip me until I bruise. Death is a sun too. A dark star casting beams of shaded starlight. I've never been touched by a sun like that. Dreaming of dissolving into a black sun. But spirits don't dream. More like phantom pains, without pain, of a mind that thought.

II. My first apartment after death was the grave.
    square footage: 63,800,000
    rent: 0$
It came unfurnished when I moved in and stayed that way until I moved on. Furniture is nonsense. Furniture is for the living. Space is for the dead.

I didn't think about my neighbors when I said I wanted to be buried in the sea. There are many spirits in the ocean. We wander the seabed with the other strange, lonely creatures inhabiting the deep.

III. Death is Nothing. There is no heaven or hell here. Just me. There is no ambition here, just inky silence that rolls out above and below, within and without. No skin, walls, or boundaries. Just nothingness with a smattering of stars that don't turn. Moonless. Sunless. Space. I do miss the moon.

I spent time as a shade in the gardens of night, wandering in fields of narcissus, their petals melting into a Sea of gold and bone. No food but the flowers. No yesterdays or afternoons. Black trees with black bark born of black soil. Blackness is so pleasing. Always with its soft coolness. I sense it without having skin: branches spindly and curling. Fruit black like obsidian, bulging from soft edges in the bark. They are so beautiful and I cannot eat them. I want to touch one. I want to rub it because I know it's exquisite. Even in death I have a taste for the exquisite.

Taste. What a dream. O dreams, whirlpools of night. With no body to wrench me into the suns day and no lungs to breathe, I can finally drown in the embrace of moonless nights. She keeps tangling her fingers in my spirit, spilling into my mouth. I want to melt into her and I realize I already have melted into her and I am the night and we are the night and we dance slowly in circles in a place with no music and a place with no time. I am held with no form and every spin feels like an orbit and with every turn some world, somewhere, a child is born and another spirit fruit forms and a bell chimes and a conch blows.

IV. I ride a white fox and sit behind the veil. Not *a* veil, *the* veil. You can hear the fox laugh in the staccato shivering noises palm fronds make when the wind blows. We ride the wind. This is the only living impulse of mine that survived death: going fast to feel a breeze.

Yoga is preparation for death. I thank the gods there is still yoga in death. In death, I inherited a horse, a fox, and a swan. Or, they just followed me to the other side. The details are minor and irrelevant.

If you would like to reach me, be still. Learn how to meditate so you can feel the entirety of presence. I am dead and present at the same time. Some people leave coins and other objects in the middle of crossroads. *How thoughtful.* I'd rather you make an altar of Me and get on your knees. Ah, there goes the ghost of my ego. It wanders every now and then. It, too, is minor and irrelevant.

V. Earth. How precious. Humanity. How troubled. Even in death I am still in love. Even in death I see beyond. If I had eyes, they'd water and weep. If I had a heart, it'd swell and beat. If only I could blanket the world in my love. If you remember nothing else, remember this: There is no death, there is only love. Everything else is an illusion.

This precious marble of a rock keeps spinning and spinning.

VI. Dear Living,

May you cross the ocean of suffering and may your time on earth be pleasurable. There's nothing to fear in death if you lived heart first. It's foolish to think salvation comes after death. What you do in this life follows you in the next. So prepare today for what you want tomorrow.

Dear Living, I watch you with a slow tenderness from beyond. I watch from beyond the veil with love and concern. I watch because I cannot touch. Maybe I could make that picture on the wall you love so much fall over and shatter the glass on the floorboards. Spirits that haunt only want attention. Are they really demons? They are no different from the living.

Dear Living, give me the stars in your eyes and I'll weave you a galaxy. I want you to use my life as an excuse to finally live. May you have the courage to keep dreaming. There is no living, there is only dreaming and nightmaring with your eyes open. Even in death, I still dream.

A Eulogy for Spring

The death of spring is an auspicious day, especially if you live near the sea. Spring died this year during the month of June in the year 2020. 2020 was a bad year for her. She didn't deserve to go out with the plague. That and I never loved her like I loved Summer was enough to do her in. She deserved better.

Nobody knew how to bring the sun out quite like her. Nobody did warm quite like her either. She wasn't a blazing bonfire like Summer but she was warm and comforting like a fireplace. In that way, I guess you could say, I needed **-we** needed- her, especially after rougher winters. Nobody arranged flowers like her either. Spring was something of a master florist.

The death of Spring came in eruption. Not such une petite mort. It was eruptive and blossoming. It was the beginning of something wonderful. I know funerals are always sad but I don't care if she's ended because all I can think about is *next*. That is her legacy: And Now....

Her death is the longest brightest day of this year. I've always frustrated myself trying to live up to it. If you wanted a second chance, better call Spring -at least that's what friends always said about her.

Today is for the Sun. Let the moon bury Spring because today we play. Spring dies so we can roll around in the flower bed of her grave. I want to faceplant into her flower. There's no better place to get rowdy than a funeral. Time for the beach bonfire. Time for sand on skin on skin. Never forgetting Our Lady of the Gardens, let us break bread in Her honor, giving and getting pleasure in Her name.

Spring, may you always come back to us.

A Eulogy for Summer

Summer is for lovers. Summer is for moving across the country in the middle of the night and not telling anyone. Summer is for thunder and lightning, bone dry heat, and fire. Summer never stayed long enough. Summer is the one who got away.

I don't know what your experiences with her were like. I thought about her all the time but mostly during winter. She was the one I could never say no to. She was a combination of hopes, dreams, and pride that peaked in an orgy of flowers and bees, honey and sun. Mother of Hedonism. She taught me so much about love and life, play and pleasure. She's something I wanted to indulge in every day of the year and when she died something inside me broke. When they said she wouldn't be here, that we couldn't go outside to meet her before her last day on earth, I crumbled.

An Ode to Death

Our Lady of Pale Moonlight, hallowed be thy name. We seek you between the sheets, in every city, and in every breath. Every move is a little death. Our Lady of Blood and Iron, of guns and switchblades. Mother of the cities and streets, drop your velvet cloak over our brothers and sons and hold them tight. You, the merciful, who takes away all pain and memory in sleep. Our Lady of Fire and Quaking. The earth spasms and dies a little death. Men dig for that slick wetness until they dig too far and shatter the crust. She creaks and groans until something hisses and shifts inside her. Mother of the Void, you are the spirit of silence.

To live another day is to die another night. Behold! The death of the moon: morning. Behold! The death of the sun: twilight. She is both rock bottom and mountain peak. Death , Our Lady of Mourning, she who gives gifts of little deaths. In spring, summer, autumn, and winter she never fails us. She is the wheel of the year and the wind that blows it.

Final Thoughts

Life is absurdity. Life is beauty and terror. I am not afraid of death, I'm afraid of not living now. I'm not afraid of death and if there is no other option I'll take it standing up, eyes open.

I lied. I'm terrified of death. It bothers me when I read about it in the news. I get nauseous thinking about my parents dying or being around a body in any way. The very first time I saw a skeleton was just a picture and it haunted me. Death. The antithesis of radiance. There are some drawbacks to being a worshiper of beauty. Fear of death is one of them, until you can find a way to be present with it. There is eternal beauty in the now. That is the only way.

Death is one long sigh. If you know me, you know I love breathing. Vanessa and her pranayama. What a beautiful inhale of life I've lived. Even at the bottom of the wheel, there was always beauty. Rest assured, devotees of beauty will be taken care of in death.

I used to be visited by the ghost frequently when I was younger. They took the shapes of people trying to live their life through me because they saw light. Some days I walked as a ghost, too. Mindlessly fluttering to every sliver of light I saw in other people. Burning myself in their embers -their house fires. When you're dead, even a house fire looks like the sun.

To be alive, to be lively. That's what attracts people. To charm is to disarm but it's not the same as being genuinely excited about your life. To be healthy. To be radiant. Live life beautifully

Live life gracefully. Live life thoughtfully.

Live life pleasurably.

May all beings be well. May all beings have peace.

Acknowledgments

Grateful acknowledgment is made to Sarah & Eryvis: your encouragement as well as your personal artistic pursuits helped inspire the making of this book. Thank you Mastin for your invaluable teachings and writings that helped me claim my own power and push this book forward. Thank you Nizar, Chelsea, Adonis, James, Anaïs, and Audre: without your literary accomplishments, I would not be the writer I am today. Lastly, I'd like to acknowledge and thank Meshell: without our years of work together, this book would not exist.

About the Author

Vanessa Dove is a yoga teacher, writer, and publishing agent based in California. She has been writing and reading since the age of 5 and likes literature about philosophy, Eastern spirituality, and moody poetry. She currently teaches Hatha Yoga and leads Lit Yoga rituals in Los Angeles, California. Find out more through her website at hathayogawithv.com

www.ingramcontent.com/pod-product-compliance
Lightning Source LLC
LaVergne TN
LVHW041548070426
835507LV00011B/982